"THIS BOOK BELONGS TO"

"ਗੁਰ ਕੀ ਬਾਣੀ ਸਦਾ ਹੀ ਰਾਹੁ ॥"

"GUR KI BANI SADA HEE RAAHU."

The Guru's Word is the eternal path.

Table of Contents:

Introduction

Greetings, young minds and aspiring adventurers! Prepare yourselves for an enlightening exploration into the world of Sikh festivals and celebrations. Secure your seatbelts, as we embark on a journey rich with narratives, crafts, and culinary delights.

Envision a realm filled with joyous laughter, delectable cuisine, radiant lights, and heartwarming stories – the essence encapsulated within Sikh festivals.

Together, we shall delve into the significance of Vaisakhi, Gurpurabs, Diwali, Maghi, Hola Mohalla, and Bandi Chhor Divas, unraveling the profound meanings that make these celebrations truly extraordinary.

But our journey does not end there. A plethora of engaging activities, delectable recipes, and captivating stories await your participation.

Prepare to don your curiosity cap as we commence this enlightening expedition.

1: VAISAKHI - THE HARVEST FESTIVAL

Vaisakhi is like a big, joyful party for the whole community. Imagine fields of golden wheat swaying in the breeze, ready for harvest. This is the time when farmers celebrate the abundance of the harvest season.

But that's not all! Many years ago, something incredible happened on Vaisakhi. Guru Gobind Singh, our wise Guru, did something amazing. He created the Khalsa, a group of brave and kind-hearted people who protect and help others. Isn't that amazing?

Vaisakhi is all about gratitude, sharing, and joy. It's a time to say thank you for the delicious food we have and to share with those who might not have as much.

Imagine having a big, special birthday party for someone you really look up to. That's what Gurpurabs are all about! We celebrate the birthdays of our Gurus, the wise and kind spiritual teachers who guide us.

One of our most beloved Gurus is Guru Nanak Dev Ji, who taught us to be kind and helpful. His birthday is a day filled with singing, praying, and sharing. We also celebrate the birthdays of other Gurus who taught us important lessons about love, equality, and doing good deeds.

As we celebrate these birthdays, we remember the wisdom and love our Gurus shared with us. It's a time to learn from their teachings and be better people. So, get ready for some heartwarming stories and exciting celebrations as we dive into Gurpurabs!

Diwali, also known as "Bandi Chhor Divas," is a dazzling festival of lights. It's a time of year when families decorate their homes with oil lamps called "diyas" and colorful rangoli designs, creating a mesmerizing display of light and color.

But Diwali isn't just about lighting lamps; it's also a time to celebrate the triumph of good over evil. Many years ago, our sixth Guru, Guru Hargobind Ji, showed us what it means to be a true warrior and a wise leader. On this day, he was released from prison along with 52 other kings. This event symbolizes the victory of righteousness over injustice.

Imagine the air filled with the sweet aroma of homemade sweets and delicious dishes. Families come together to prepare delightful treats like "ladoos" , "jalebi", and "sevian". These scrumptious goodies are shared with friends and neighbors, spreading warmth and happiness.

Diwali is a time for prayer and reflection too. Families visit the Gurdwara to seek the blessings of the Guru and offer their gratitude.

Lohri, the Festival of Bonfires, is another exciting celebration cherished by Sikhs. It's a festival that brings warmth and joy during the chilly winter months.

Lohri is celebrated, usually on the 13th of January each year. Families eagerly await this day, much like you eagerly anticipate a fun day at the park.

Centuries ago, there lived a man named Dulla Bhatti. He was a true hero and a savior of the poor. During the reign of Emperor Akbar, Dulla Bhatti rescued young girls who were being taken away forcibly and provided them with a safe home. He was like a beacon of hope, spreading light and love in the world.

Sikhs celebrate Lohri to remember this brave and kind-hearted man. Lohri is a time when families come together around a bonfire, just like gathering around a campfire during a camping trip.

They sing joyful songs, tell stories, and toss sesame seeds, jaggery, and popcorn into the fire as a symbol of letting go of the old and embracing the new.

5: MAGHI - THE WINTER FESTIVAL

Brrr, winter is here, and it's time to cozy up and celebrate Maghi, the Sikh winter festival! Just imagine the world outside covered in a soft, white blanket of snow, and everyone gathering around a toasty bonfire. Maghi is a day to remember the bravery and courage of the Chali Mukte, 40 fearless Sikhs who stood up for what they believed in. They showed incredible strength during a battle against a mighty army. Even though they were outnumbered, they didn't give up. This day is all about honoring their valor.

As the sun rises on Maghi, families light oil lamps and candles to chase away the winter darkness. It's like a beacon of warmth and hope in the cold season. People also visit the Gurdwara to hear stories about the Chali Mukte and seek inspiration for their own lives.

But what's a celebration without delicious food? For Maghi, people enjoy hearty winter dishes like "saag" and "makki di roti". These warm and filling foods are perfect for keeping you cozy on chilly days.

And here's a fun fact: On Maghi morning, some Sikhs take a dip in holy rivers like the Ganges to cleanse their souls. It's a refreshing and spiritual experience that connects them with nature and their faith.

Hola Mohalla is like a grand carnival, full of excitement and bravery! It's celebrated with incredible energy and enthusiasm, making it one of the most exciting Sikh festivals.

Picture this: colorful processions fill the streets, people wearing dazzling costumes, and martial arts displays that will leave you in awe. It's a day when Sikhs come together to show their strength and warrior spirit. The word "Hola" means "hall" or "challenge," and "Mohalla" means "an organized procession." So, Hola Mohalla is all about facing challenges and showing what you're made of, just like a superhero! On this special day, Sikhs perform "gatka," a traditional martial art. It's like watching a thrilling dance with swords, sticks, and shields. You'll be amazed by the skill and precision of the performers.

And that's not all! There are exciting horse-riding competitions where riders display their equestrian skills. It's a bit like a race, but with a touch of bravery and style. During Hola Mohalla, langars (community meals) are served to all visitors. These meals are open to everyone, regardless of their background, which shows the importance of equality and sharing in Sikhism.

HUNGRY YET? GET READY FOR A CULINARY JOURNEY FILLED WITH DELICIOUSNESS! SIKH FESTIVALS ARE NOT ONLY ABOUT STORIES AND CELEBRATIONS; THEY ALSO BRING MOUTHWATERING TREATS THAT'LL TICKLE YOUR TASTE BUDS.

Vaisakhi Treat: Pinni

Vaisakhi, the harvest festival, is all about celebrating the bounty of nature. And what better way to celebrate than with a sweet treat like "Pinni"? These little round sweets are like bites of sunshine, filled with warmth and love.

Ingredients:

- 1 cup whole wheat flour
- 1/2 cup ghee (clarified butter)
- 1/2 cup crushed jaggery (or brown sugar)
- A handful of chopped almonds, pistachios, and cashews
- A pinch of cardamom powder

Instructions:

1. Heat ghee in a pan and add the whole wheat flour. Roast it until it turns golden brown and smells heavenly.
2. Add the crushed jaggery and mix until it melts and blends with the flour.
3. Toss in the chopped nuts and cardamom powder. Stir well.
4. Turn off the heat and let it cool slightly.
5. While the mixture is still warm, shape it into small round balls or patties.
6. Let them cool completely, and your Pinnis are ready to enjoy!

Diwali Delight: Ladoos

Diwali, the festival of lights, deserves a sweet treat that's as bright and delightful as the festival itself. Enter "Ladoos"! These round, sweet balls are like little bundles of happiness.

Ingredients:
- 1 cup besan (gram flour)
- 1/4 cup ghee (clarified butter)
- 1/2 cup powdered sugar
- A handful of chopped nuts (cashews, almonds, pistachios)
- A pinch of cardamom powder

Instructions:
1. Heat ghee in a pan and add the besan (gram flour). Roast it on low heat until it turns aromatic and golden brown.
2. Add the chopped nuts and cardamom powder. Mix well.
3. Turn off the heat and let it cool slightly.
4. Gradually add the powdered sugar and mix until everything comes together.
5. While the mixture is still warm, shape it into round ladoos.
6. Let them cool completely, and your Ladoos are ready to share and savor!

Sikh festivals are not just about rituals and stories; they're about coming together as a family to create wonderful memories. Let's explore how families celebrate these festivals with love, togetherness, and joyful traditions.

Decorating the Home

Festivals are the perfect time to turn your home into a colorful wonderland. Families work together to decorate their houses with vibrant rangoli patterns, twinkling lights, and beautiful garlands. It's like turning your home into a magical palace!

Cooking Up a Storm

In the kitchen, it's a flurry of activity. Parents and children team up to prepare delicious festival foods. Whether it's kneading dough for rotis, frying jalebis, or making ladoos, the kitchen becomes a place of laughter, learning, and the aroma of mouthwatering dishes.

Visiting the Gurdwara

Families gather at the Gurdwara, the Sikh place of worship, to offer prayers, listen to hymns (kirtan), and seek the blessings of the Guru.

Participating in Nagar Kirtan
During festivals like Vaisakhi, families join Nagar Kirtan processions. These vibrant parades move through the streets, with the Guru Granth Sahib (our holy scripture) carried in a beautifully decorated float. Families sing hymns and distribute snacks and drinks to the crowds, spreading joy along the way.

Giving Back: Sewa
One of the most beautiful aspects of Sikh festivals is "sewa," or selfless service. Families come together to prepare and serve meals at the langar (community kitchen) in the Gurdwara. It's a way of giving back to the community and teaching children the value of helping others.

Creating Memories
Festivals are a time for creating lasting memories. Whether it's lighting fireworks on Diwali, competing in a horse race on Hola Mohalla, or sharing a meal with neighbors, families treasure these moments of love, unity, and joy.

These family traditions make Sikh festivals extra special. They strengthen bonds and teach important values.

What's better than one festival?

Many festivals! And to keep track of all the exciting Sikh festivals, we have a special tool - a festival calendar! In this chapter, we'll explore a calendar that will help you stay updated on the important dates of Sikh festivals for the upcoming year.

Why a Festival Calendar?

A festival calendar is like a treasure map, guiding you to the most joyous and meaningful celebrations throughout the year. It helps you plan your participation and make the most of each festival.

Important Sikh Festivals

Let's take a look at some of the key Sikh festivals you'll find on the calendar:

1. **Vaisakhi:** Celebrated on April 13 or 14, Vaisakhi marks the Sikh New Year and the creation of the Khalsa. It's a time for harvest celebrations and joyful processions.
2. **Diwali:** Falling in October or November, Diwali, also known as Bandi Chhor Divas, is the Festival of Lights. It celebrates the release of Guru Hargobind Ji from prison.
3. **Maghi:** Occurring in January, Maghi is the Sikh winter festival. It's a time for community gatherings and remembering the Chali Mukte.
4. **Hola Mohalla:** This festival follows Holi and usually takes place in March. It's a time for martial arts displays, processions, and community service.
5. **Gurpurabs:** These are the birthdays of Sikh Gurus and are celebrated with prayers, hymns, and community meals. Guru Nanak Dev Ji's Gurpurab, for instance, falls in November.

10: GLOSSARY OF TERMS

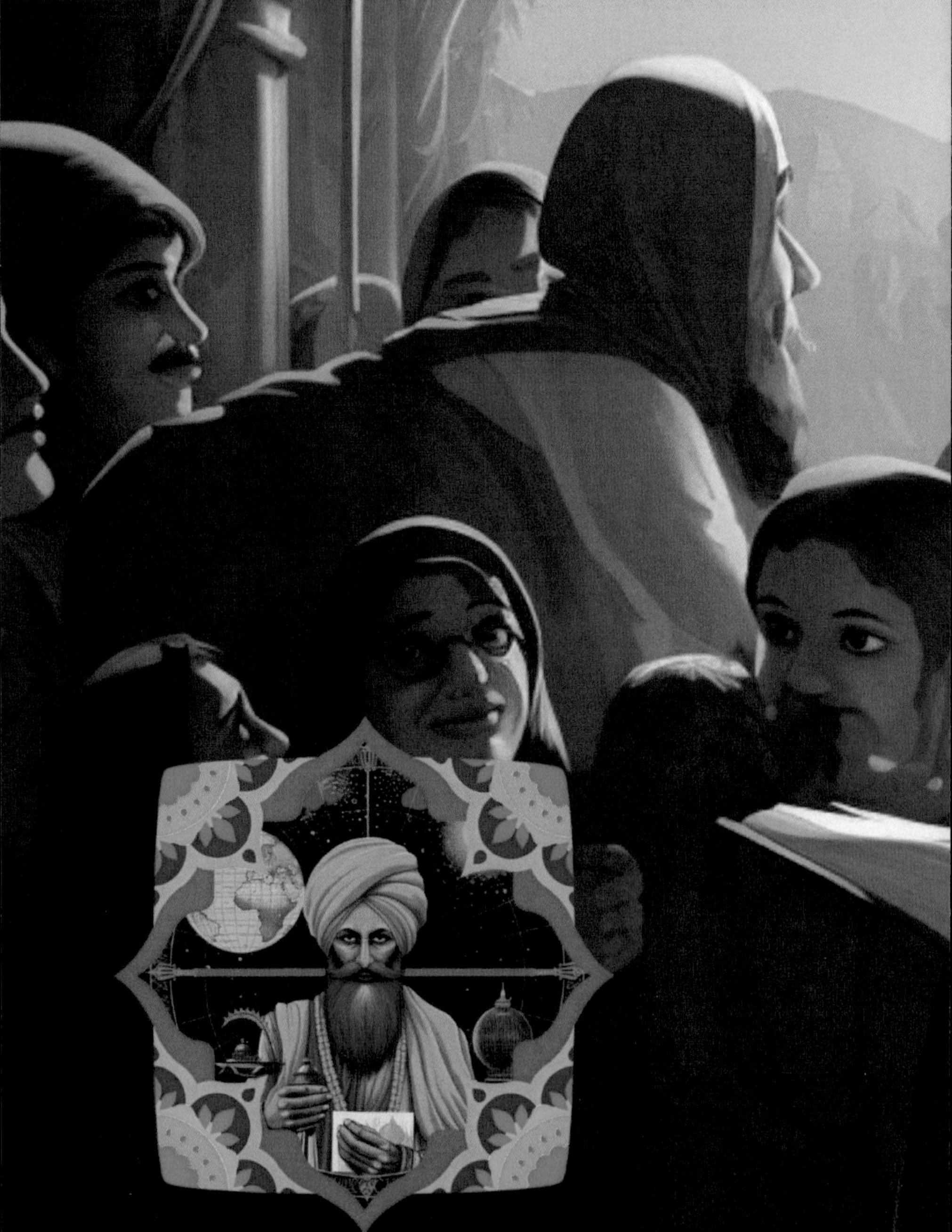

Welcome to your very own Sikh Festival Glossary! Sometimes, when we explore new worlds, we come across words we don't know. That's where a glossary comes in handy. In this chapter, we'll discover the meanings of Sikh terms, Punjabi words, and festival-related vocabulary.

Sikh Terms:

1. **Guru:** A spiritual teacher and leader in Sikhism, who guides and inspires followers on their spiritual journey.
2. **Gurdwara:** The place of worship for Sikhs, where they come together for prayers, hymns, and community meals (langar).
3. **Khalsa:** A community of initiated Sikhs who follow the Sikh Code of Conduct. They are known for their bravery, purity, and commitment to Sikh values.
4. **Sewa:** Selfless service or volunteering for the community. It's a core principle in Sikhism.
5. **Langar:** A community kitchen in the Gurdwara where free meals are served to everyone, regardless of their background.

Punjabi Words:

1. **Saag:** Spiced mustard greens, a popular Punjabi dish often enjoyed during festivals.
2. **Makki di Roti:** Cornflat bread, typically eaten with saag during the winter festival of Maghi.
3. **Jalebi:** A sticky, sweet dessert made by deep-frying batter into pretzel-like shapes and soaking them in sugar syrup.
4. **Sevian:** A sweet vermicelli dessert, often prepared during Diwali and other festive occasions.
5. **Pinni:** A sweet treat made from flour, ghee, and jaggery, enjoyed during Vaisakhi.

Fun Facts:

- **Young Guru: Guru Gobind Singh Ji became the 10th Guru at just 9 years old!**
- **Sikh Poetry: He was a skilled poet, and his verses still inspire today.**
- **Brave Sons: The Chaar Sahibzaade were Guru Gobind Singh's four fearless sons.**
- **Khalsa's Five K's: The five K's symbolize Sikh principles, like courage and faith.**
- **Panj Pyare Origins: The Panj Pyare hailed from diverse parts of India.**
- **Equality: Sikhism promotes equality regardless of caste, creed, or gender.**
- **The Turban: Sikhs wear turbans proudly, a symbol of their faith.**
- **Harmandir Sahib's Gold: The Harmandir Sahib, or Golden Temple, is adorned with over 160 kg of gold, symbolizing the spiritual and material wealth of Sikhism.**

- **Golden Temple Visitors:** Over 100,000 daily visitors make the Golden Temple in Amritsar a global pilgrimage site.
- **Largest Community Kitchen:** The Golden Temple's langar serves 100,000+ free meals daily, driven by volunteer efforts.
- **Global Sikh Presence:** Sikhs constitute 2% of India's population (30 million globally) with a significant diaspora in the UK, Canada, and the US.
- **Gurmukhi Script:** Sikh scriptures are in Gurmukhi, a script created by Guru Angad Dev Ji, the second Sikh Guru.
- **Amrit Ceremony:** It marks initiation into the Khalsa brotherhood.
- **Selfless Service:** Sikhs serve free meals in langars, open to all.
- **Baisakhi:** Sikhs celebrate the New Year on Baisakhi
- **No Priesthood:** There are no priests or clergy in Sikhism.
- **Interfaith Harmony:** Sikhism actively promotes interfaith dialogue and collaboration.
- **Khanda Symbolism:** The Khanda, a central Sikh symbol, represents the oneness of God, truth, and the creative power of the divine.
- **Sikh Turban Records:** Sikhs are known for their distinctive turbans, with the Guinness World Record for the largest turban set at a staggering 400 meters in length.

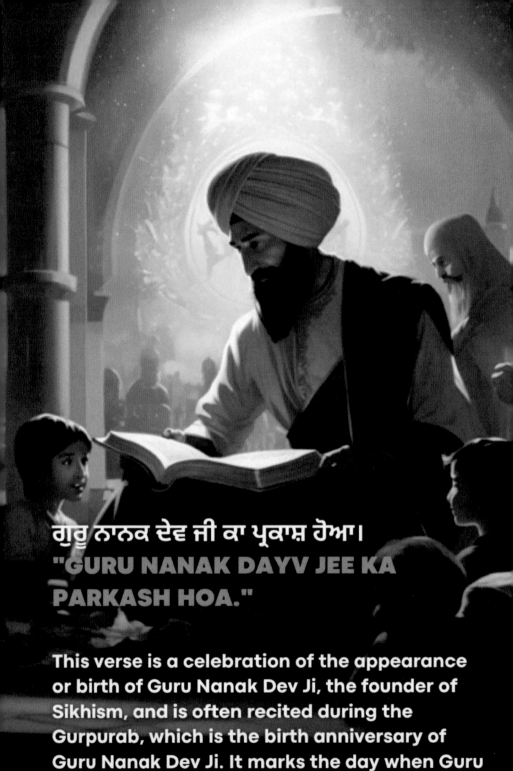

ਗੁਰੂ ਨਾਨਕ ਦੇਵ ਜੀ ਕਾ ਪ੍ਰਕਾਸ਼ ਹੋਆ।
"GURU NANAK DAYV JEE KA
PARKASH HOA."

This verse is a celebration of the appearance
or birth of Guru Nanak Dev Ji, the founder of
Sikhism, and is often recited during the
Gurpurab, which is the birth anniversary of
Guru Nanak Dev Ji. It marks the day when Guru
Nanak's divine light entered the world.

Dear Reader,
I hope this book has been a delightful journey through the vibrant world of Sikh festivals and celebrations. I want to extend my heartfelt gratitude to you for being a part of this adventure.

Sikhi for Young Minds is a series that aims to make learning about Sikhism a joyful and enriching experience for young readers like you. Through these books, we hope to inspire curiosity, foster understanding, and celebrate the beautiful tapestry of Sikh culture.

As you continue your journey, remember that the spirit of Sikh festivals—of love, unity, and selfless service—is something you can carry with you in your heart always. Embrace the values and lessons you've discovered in this book, and let them guide you to be a compassionate and caring individual.

Thank you for being a part of the Sikhi for Young Minds series. Your curiosity and enthusiasm are the driving forces behind our mission to share knowledge and celebrate diversity.

Wishing you a world filled with understanding, respect, and the joy of discovery.
Warm regards,

Manav Singh Chadha

Made in the USA
Monee, IL
04 December 2024